FR
of JESUS
A LENTEN
MEDITATION

Fr Philip Caldwell

*All booklets are published
thanks to the generous support of the
members of the Catholic Truth Society*

First published 2025 by The Incorporated Catholic Truth Society
40-46 Harleyford Road London SE11 5AY Tel: 020 7640 0042
Fax: 020 7640 0040 0040 www.ctsbooks.org

ISBN 978 1 78469 835 5

All biblical quotations are taken from the Jerusalem Bible, except where noted.

CONTENTS

PREFACE

This little booklet has been put together as a five-week retreat for Lent. Comprising a combination of biblical meditations, passages for prayerful reflection, and questions to stimulate consideration or discussion, it was first delivered to the Sisters of Mercy in Sunderland, as a preached retreat. Now, it has been shaped to help lead you on a spiritual journey through this season according to a particular theme. It might be used individually or in a group. Each section begins with a longer meditation which could be read at the weekend, when perhaps you have more time, and returned to for prayerful reflection during the week, when perhaps you have less. Using the Daily Meditation Guide, choose some points from the opening reflection and one of the scriptural passages referenced. Some questions will also be given to stimulate your consideration or discussion. The pattern for each of the five weeks is the same – offering, I hope enough structure for you to develop a rhythm, but loose enough for you to adapt in a way that suits you best. The booklet can be used in conjunction with some podcasts, and the artwork it contains is also meant as stimulus to prayer. I hope you'll find it user-friendly, and through it come to a deeper knowledge of your faith and to an experience of the friendship of Jesus.

A Lenten Journey of Friendship
with Jesus Christ

Let me tell you how I made his acquaintance.
I had heard much of him, but took no heed.
He sent daily gifts and presents, but I never thanked him.
He often seemed to want my friendship, but I remained
cold... At last he crossed my path and with tears in his eyes
he besought me saying, come and abide with me.

(Robert Hugh Benson)

It didn't take me long to decide on an approach for this do-it-yourself retreat. I'm sure everyone wants the same thing from this blessed time of Lent – to come closer to Jesus, to be one with Him as He lives out the days of His Passion in the loving gaze of His Father. And that's why for me, and I hope for you, there can be only one way of approach that will satisfy. It could never be enough, would never do, if all we wanted was to spend this time trying to be better: to be a more active servant, harder worker, attentive helper, more devoted in prayer – no, our desire to come close to Jesus, and to have made known to us everything He has learned from His Father, can only be satisfied if in these days each one of us hears Him call us friend. And if, as a result, our soul begins to sing with the lines of that Lenten hymn, 'But O! my Friend, my Friend indeed' then we might just begin to grasp that our need to love and to be loved was the need for which He spent His life. That's why these days must be days of friendship, with each other and with the Lord.

If there is anything clear in the Gospels it is this: that Jesus Christ, first and foremost, desires our friendship. He can press a servant, command a worker, be rightfully expectant of a sister or brother, urge a helper – but a friend He can only love, and hope that our service, our work, and our help is freely given because of the love we enjoy. So, just for these few days let's try to forget who we feel we should be, how we might be expected to behave and what we must do – and let's try to enter that moment when first we felt the love not of a Master or Teacher but a Friend.

It is moments of friendship in the Gospels, above all others, that endear Jesus to us – moments in which He reveals Himself as One who is as hungry for our love as we are for His – hungrier in fact. As we will experience this Lent, and see especially in the coming days of His Passion, it is when Jesus is 'lifted up' in all His human need, that we glimpse His divine glory, and feel the attraction and strength of His love. We know of His great works of power and these draw out our admiration and awe: but when we hear of how He sat down weary by the well-side, while His friends went off for food, and of how He asked a woman there for a drink; and when we remember that He 'loved Martha, and her sister Mary, and Lazarus' and that He looked steadily at the rich young man and loved him, too;

then we hear of a Friend who is calling out to His own. We are His own and, in these days, we want to hear His call and receive Him: 'Look, I am standing at the door, knocking. If one of you hears me calling and opens the door, I will come in to share his meal, side by side with him.' (*Rev* 3:20).

In his wonderful book, *The Friendship of Christ*, the English priest, Robert Hugh Benson, speaks about how our relationships begin to take shape:

> Human friendships normally have their beginning in some small external detail. We catch a phrase, we hear a certain inflection of the voice – we notice the look of the eyes or a movement in walking, and that tiny experience seems to us like the initiation of a whole new world. We take the little event as a symbol of a universe that lies behind; we think we have detected a soul exactly suited to our own, a temperament which either from its resemblance to our own, or from a harmonious dissimilarity, is precisely fitted to be our companion. Then the process of friendship begins; we exhibit our own characteristics; we examine his: in point after point, we find what we expected to find, and we verify our guesses; and he too, no less, follows the same method until that point is reached.

'That point' is one of happy surrender or cautious retreat.

To explain this better, perhaps I could tell you of my first meeting with an old couple, now dead, with whom I became good friends. In 1994, I was a deacon on a pastoral placement, preparing for priestly ordination, and to be honest, I wasn't at all sure about the life on which I was about to embark. It was July, but the weather was dull, and I had to make my first visit to a housebound woman in a run-down part of town. Very nervous, I knocked at the door – no response. Thinking she'd been taken into hospital, I decided to bang loudly once more and be satisfied that my duty was done. The door opened, so I went in, slowly. Before me was a man, sat in an armchair. He was behind a newspaper, holding a mug of tea and a cigarette. In the middle of the room, there was an upright vacuum cleaner with its engine running loudly. After a moment or two, he said, ''Ave you come to see Mary?' He was shouting over the hoover. 'I'll turn that thing off in a minute and take you up. You see, Father, it does her a world of good, thinking I'm cleaning up down here!'

In bed upstairs was his dying wife. I had brought her Communion, but after the prayers I found that I couldn't get the top of the pyx off. As I struggled, she peacefully smoothed the covers with her hand and said, 'I had all my five babies in this bed – everyone a joy. Tek yer time, love, I'm happy waiting here for Our Lord.' Still I couldn't open it. 'Eee, haven't you got lovely teeth,' she said smiling and showing she'd not one in her head. Once she'd received Holy Communion, she lay back on the pillow, praying for a few minutes, and then, with a beautiful, toothless grin she said: 'When you go down, Father, tell that clown I do love him, but he's fooling no one with the hoover.'

I'm not sure if it was her gesture of stroking the bed, the hoover that somehow seemed to symbolise their love, or the inflection of their broad Lancashire accents that made my heart go out to them in friendship and love.

The divine friendship – the way in which we come to know Jesus, and in which we realise how and why He seeks to know us – is no different. We can hear in the Gospels the inflection of His voice: 'Martha, Martha', or catch His playful phrase, 'and you a teacher in Israel and you don't know these things!' We can hear of Him looking steadily and lovingly and of the many gestures and symbols that He uses to evoke the love of His friends.

But in the days of the Passion, with what love He addresses us through His friends! How much more acutely do we hear His inflection when He says: 'Mary!' to His bereft friend at the tomb (*John* 20:16). How more poignant is the phrase, 'Friend, why are you here?' when addressed to the Judas who kisses Him in the garden (*Matt* 26:50, RSV)? How loving is the gaze which meets the eyes of His friend Peter in the courtyard (*Luke* 22:61)? How moving His gesture of washing feet in the Cenacle (*John* 13:1-17)? From all these details, we build up a picture of our Friend. But not only that; in the gestures, the words, and tone of speech of His friends, we begin to see how we might act and speak in His company, begin to grasp what attracts

Him, draws Him out, and wins Him. You can learn a lot about a person from their friends.

In this little retreat together, I thought we might contemplate the friends of Jesus – how the Lord shows Himself a Friend to them and they to Him. I thought we might take a few figures each day and try to put ourselves in their place so that we might experience the friendship of the Lord through them, and so come to know Him more clearly and love Him more dearly ourselves.

Even if you've never drawn it up, you've probably all got a personal list of favourite Gospel figures. Obviously, Jesus tops the chart as everybody's number one, but other favourites might be a surprise. A few years ago, a human rights worker from South America, a friend of St Oscar Romero, came to give a talk at the college where I was working. She was in England to give the annual Cafod Lecture. There was a chance for questions after her address and someone asked who her favourite character in the Scriptures was. In a very moving way, she explained that Nicodemus was her personal favourite because she could identify with him. Quite often, she said, her work involved recovering the tortured bodies of the disappeared, returning them to their families, and burying them.

Identifying ourselves with the characters of the Passion narrative has a long tradition in the Church. Selecting who we prefer and why, and attempting to make a deeply personal identification with someone, can help us to unfold the mysteries we celebrate in these days. This is because in such an identification there is the realisation that we are not merely connecting with someone from the past, real or imagined, but also with each other; we are recognising the truth about our humanity, about ourselves in the light of the Gospel. Somehow, I could recognise a bond of friendship with a stranger from South America because we both found the truth about ourselves in Nicodemus. He shared a place in my top ten, too, not because he reverently buried the body of Jesus, but because he went to Jesus by night – a proud teacher, shaky in faith, concerned about his reputation, and reluctant to commit. Our motives were different, but through Nicodemus we both experienced the gentle loving friendship of our Lord, heard His voice, and felt His presence now. In that Gospel figure, a brother and sister could find a place of truth that brings communion.

So, as we begin this sacred season, let's commit ourselves to deeper friendship with Jesus. Let's frequent the places where He goes, seek out His friends, and get to know His ways. Let's reveal ourselves to Him as if for the first time; say and do all that we need in order to renew our friendship with Him again. Because in these days, we will discover a Friend who invites us to His table to drink His wine, who washes our feet, lies peacefully next to us, is with us in fear and darkness, dies forgiving us and rises to say He will be with us always. What a privileged time, this time of friendship we can have together.

Daily Meditation Guide

Suggested time for prayer: thirty minutes

Preparation

1   Choose one of the scriptural passages from the week's reflection.
2   Read the scriptural text through a couple of times, slowly.

Prayer

1   Imagine yourself on your way to meet a friend – briefly rehearse the meeting.
2   Pray to the Holy Spirit to enable you to enter the passage and encounter the Word.
3   What is God saying to you today?
4   What do you desire from your encounter?

Passage

1   What do you notice most in this passage?
2   To whom do you feel drawn in this story?
3   What speaks to you most here?

Praise

1   Take some time to thank God for your friendship with Jesus and to note what you have experienced today.

Week One:
Three Lenten Women of Prayer, Fasting, and Almsgiving

We have said that you can tell a lot from someone's friends. Generally, that means that a person's friends teach you about that person, what they're like, and what one might expect. Simon the Leper decides that Jesus is no wise man or prophet because He allows a woman with a certain reputation to anoint Him, kiss Him, and wipe His feet with her hair (*Luke* 7:36-50). Because Jesus welcomes these actions with gratitude and love, Simon wonders what kind of man Jesus is. He makes friends with tax collectors and sinners!

The three women that I'd like to contemplate today all make gestures that the Lord notices and receives. They act in a way that He welcomes, and to which He responds. They have a certain way, a graciousness that engages and pleases Him. There is something about these women that draws them to Jesus, but that also draws Jesus to them – something about them that singles them out in His sight. In a way, they're appropriate for Lent, these three. One's gestures are prayerful; we might say another's are born out of fasting; and the last makes a generous gesture of almsgiving. These are the type of friends that Jesus wants – people who are open, attentive, and willing to give. We'll see that they're not the usual types; that they have their troubles, but they're people who have caught His eye and through their words and actions graciously introduce us to their friend.

The Mother of Zebedee's Sons (*Matt* 20:20-28) – A Woman of Prayerful Approach

The first woman that I've chosen is the mother of Zebedee's sons. Perhaps not someone we would immediately think of as a friend of Jesus – and yet, though she's without name in the Gospel and is only mentioned twice, she is in the company of Jesus more than we might think. What is it that draws them together? Well, let's see.

At first, she seems quite unpromising: there's not a lot to go on, and what we have tradition has interpreted negatively: presenting a pushy woman who is quick to promise, over-eager and unprepared. Then again, all of that seems to fit with how Lent tends to go – given my past performances in these forty days, tradition would identify me as a pretty unpromising bet: each Ash Wednesday, I've not a lot to go on, I am eager but unprepared. As a Lenten figure, I feel we might identify with this woman pretty well – she's human and real, but offers hidden spiritual depths of a kind I'd like to reach. When you contemplate her further and make one or two connections, this apparent nobody emerges as a woman of prayer and a true disciple.

Just in case there should be any doubt as to the truth

of my claims for Zebedee's wife, I checked her out against the *Catechism* which identifies adoration, petition, intercession, and praise as the essential qualities of prayer.

Well, she approaches Jesus and 'bows low'. There is only one other place in the Gospels where a mother appeals on behalf of a child and she too is described as bowing low. It's the Canaanite woman whose daughter is sick, and to her Jesus says: 'Woman, you have great faith' (*Matt* 15:21-28). Would it be wrong, then, to see such faith-filled reverence in the low bow of the mother of Zebedee's sons? Does she not, in her own way, adore Jesus? Might it be this quiet prayerful gesture that first inclines Him to her? Certainly, she petitions Him. The *Catechism* gives this definition of petitionary prayer:

> Christian petition is centred on the desire and search for the Kingdom to come, in keeping with the teaching of Christ. There is a hierarchy in these petitions: we pray first for the Kingdom, then for what is necessary to welcome it and co-operate with its coming. This collaboration with the mission of Christ and the Holy Spirit, which is now that of the Church, is the object of the prayer of the apostolic community (*CCC* 2632).

According to the *Catechism*, then, could we deny a place in the apostolic community of prayer to a woman who petitions: 'Promise that these two sons of mine may sit one at your right hand and the other at your left in your

Kingdom'? You might claim she's misguided, but her desire is for the Kingdom, and what's more, she will do what is necessary to collaborate with its coming. Along with her sons, she consents to drink the cup, the suffering of the wrath of God. Some exegetes would have us believe that only the sons say 'yes' to that cup, which is a communion with the blood of Christ. But what then of Chapter 27 in the same Gospel, which describes the death of Jesus? Who do we find has remained faithful throughout the mission of Christ and is a friend unto death?

> And many women were there, watching from a distance, the same women who had followed Jesus from Galilee and looked after him. Among them were Mary of Magdala, Mary the mother of James and Joseph, and the mother of Zebedee's sons (*Matt* 27:55).

I wonder, was it her low bow, perhaps her self-effacing nature, her love for her sons, or even her over-eager request which first sealed their friendship? Because this is a woman who doesn't come and go – this is a woman who has remained with Jesus, looked after Him, and stayed with Him all the way to the Cross. Perhaps you could consider taking her approach to Jesus in prayer today.

So she is an example of adoration and of the prayer of true petition that desires the Kingdom and faithfully collaborates in its coming. But what of intercession and praise? The *Catechism* says:

Since Abraham, intercession – asking on behalf of another – has been characteristic of a heart attuned to God's mercy. In intercession, the one who prays looks not only to his or her own interests but also to the interests of others (*CCC* 2635).

'What is it you want?' Jesus asks her, but she asks only for 'these two sons of mine'. I won't push the passage to find an example of praise – that this woman is an unexpected friend of Jesus who comes close to him through prayer, seems clear enough.

On Ash Wednesday, the Gospel warned us to be careful not to parade our good deeds, to be humble, and to pray in secret. I think why I'm ultimately attracted to the mother of Zebedee's sons as a friend is that despite all my prejudices, despite our constant misinterpretation of her words and deeds, for two thousand years she has prayed from her secret place in the Gospel that the seats that the Father has allotted to us in Christ will be filled.

If you want a humble, human and determined fellow disciple to stay with you in prayer right to the Cross of Jesus – silently willing the Kingdom – then you could do worse. Why not make friends with her?

The Woman with the Issue of Blood (*Mark* 5:25-34) – A Woman of Bold Faith

The next woman I thought we could contemplate is a woman who reaches out to Jesus in faith: the woman who has had a haemorrhage for twelve years. On one occasion, people ask Jesus why His disciples do not fast, and He says to them that while the Bridegroom is with them it would be unthinkable for them to fast – but He insists that when the Bridegroom is taken away they will fast. Jesus associates the time of fasting with His suffering and death – with His leaving; to fast is to suffer like Jesus and to wait for His return.

> Now there was a woman who had suffered a haemorrhage for twelve years; after long and painful treatment under various doctors, she had spent all she had without being any the better for it, in fact, she was getting worse (*Mark* 5:25-27).

'Now there was a woman who had suffered' – this is the only time in the whole Gospel that the word 'suffer' (*paschō*) is used of anyone except Jesus. The woman's suffering, which has caused her to be rejected by her people and which has stigmatised and humiliated her, is identified with the sufferings of Jesus. Perhaps that is what attracts Jesus to this woman – perhaps He sees something of Himself in her and at once loves her by empathising with her situation and experiences. This woman's suffering has been like a fast: a fast from human company and tenderness, a fast from people and property, a fast from all that gave her self-respect. But this fast ends when the Bridegroom returns.

As you know better than me, in the spiritual classics the soul is often represented as the bride who waits for her bridegroom to come and consummate their love. The soul fasts and suffers while it waits – it experiences the darkness of separation and is sick with longing. Whether we 'suffer' physically or spiritually, we can identify with this woman and we can learn from her bold gesture of faith how to be a friend of Jesus. Perhaps what makes this woman bold in her gesture is that she feels she has nothing else to lose – she's already depleted economically, emotionally and socially. What else can she lose? We should be mindful of how impossible her situation is and how immediate and complete her cure. In this transformation our friend offers us hope.

We might sit today and contemplate ourselves as cut off from Jesus by the bustle of life and by our own weakness, sickness and sin. We might imagine the sense of separation and isolation this woman knows, and which maybe we have known in prayer for some time too. We could take time to consider slowly and in great detail the faith we have, and the gesture we would make to get our Friend's attention. Her initiative in touching Jesus, without even a word of request, is unique in the Gospels. We might contemplate the face of Jesus as He turns to us and says, 'Who touched me?' We might imagine how suddenly all our difficulties and our silence might be broken by this loving gesture of ours, and how once we have gained our Friend's attention, we tell Him the whole truth. The woman in the Gospel pours out her heart to the Lord once she is certain of His saving touch. May we be inspired to reach for the Lord today and tell Him the whole truth.

The Poor Widow (*Luke* 21:1-4, *Mark* 12:41-44) – Generously Gives Herself

Only Jesus notices the poor widow. No doubt everyone else, the disciples included, were so distracted by the crowds who were giving much that they didn't notice the woman who gave all. In Mark's Gospel, this story is beautifully constructed. We're told that the 'Passover was at hand', so the city was busy with people and the rich are putting much in the treasury. Jesus's eyes are caught by this woman. Why? Well, just before, we had been warned of the scribes who like to go about in fine robes, be greeted obsequiously in the marketplaces, take the best seats in the synagogue and places of honour at banquets, who devour the property of widows, and make a show of long prayers. The self-important men are contrasted by one of the selfless women they persecute – but then again, they persecute Jesus too. Just as Jesus is willing to give His life as a ransom for many, so this woman from the little she has gives 'all she had to live on', or as the Greek literally translated says, 'gives her whole life'. The Passover that is at hand is being lived out already in this generous woman, and Jesus sees it.

No wonder Jesus calls His disciples to Himself, and in

His distinctive turn of phrase says: 'Amen I say to you. You see this widow…' He has said 'Amen' before and does so again. Whenever He does, He is speaking as a teacher who is giving a solemn lesson about the Kingdom – its coming now and in the future: 'Amen, I say to you, whoever gives a cup of water; whoever has left house or brothers or sisters…' In yet another place, again sitting and teaching, as He does here outside the treasury, Jesus calls His disciples to Himself and gives a solemn instruction. There it says:

> But Jesus called them to him and said, 'You know that among the pagans the ruler lord it over them, and their great men make their authority felt. This is not to happen among you. No; anyone who wants to be great among you must be your servant, and anyone who wants to be first among you must be your slave, just as the Son of Man came not to be served but to serve, and to give his life as a ransom for many.' (*Matt* 20:25-28).

Perhaps we don't realise what good friends of Jesus we already are. This little friend of Jesus, who does her unobtrusive work of mercy, who has no spirit of dominance or desire to be noticed within her, but seeks quietly to give her life in service, this little servant Jesus would most certainly call friend – well, He and she have so much in common. They view the world and the meaning of life in exactly the same way. Jesus can tell all that from her gesture and her two small coins.

All three women we have mentioned today become acquainted with Jesus through some simple gesture – a bow, a touch, a gift, a prayer, but in all three of these nascent friendships there is a hint of suffering. The woman with the haemorrhage has suffered for twelve years; the widow suffers to give her whole life in her two small coins; and Zebedee's wife must drink of the cup of suffering in order to collaborate with the Kingdom. The key to friendship, then, would seem to be compassion – being prepared to suffer alongside someone – that is what the Good Jesus committed Himself to do for us this week, and that is how we will become His solid friends. To show our friendship for Him we might try the gesture of one or all of these women – but the gesture only serves to call attention to something that is common to all of Jesus's friends – they are all marked with the Sign of the Cross. May He see in each of us the Sign of His Cross and recognise us as His friends.

Week Two: Three Friends Who Come by Night – Judas, Nicodemus and the Magdalene

What can we do when we feel we cannot be the friend of Jesus – when something holds us back and we can't approach Him? Unfortunately, not everyone's journey with the Lord is an easy one – we don't all walk smoothly towards the light and stay there with Him. We, most of us, struggle in the half light and shadows, sometimes we even decide to choose the darkness of sin. We're constantly betrayed by our own weakness, by our restless hearts. So how can we make sense of our sinful selves? What are we to do, when as the psalmist says, 'our one companion is darkness' (*Ps* 88:19) and we feel we cannot call the Lord Jesus our Friend? Well, we could begin by simply trusting God's word. Happily the Gospels teach us that Jesus has a friend in every place – even the darkest. We could look to some of these companions and learn something from the friendship that Jesus had with them.

Today, I'd like us to contemplate three friends of Jesus who come to Him by night: Judas, Nicodemus, and Mary Magdalene – three friends who feel they cannot meet Jesus in the full light of day. Each one is in a different position. Judas gives up a place of intimacy, close to Jesus, and chooses to turn his back and to go out into the night.

Nicodemus comes to Jesus under the cover of darkness, and their friendship is born in the night, but he lacks the courage to leave his past behind and struggles to embrace a new life in the light. And Mary? Well, it's very early in the morning and still dark when she begins her sorrowful and misguided search for her Friend among the dead.

Surely, the shades of sin that we experience in our own lives are echoed in the stories of these three. On a rare occasion, we too might have chosen to turn away to darkness like Judas, probably more often we've refused to move out into the full light like Nicodemus, and sometimes we've remained in the half-light, resisting the future, staying in the past, and nursing our disappointment and pain there like Mary. However shady we might feel our life is, or has been, we have a friend in one of these – and more importantly, through them we know that even at our darkest moment we have a Friend in Jesus.

Judas (*Matt* 26:47-56)

Can we really say that Judas, the traitor, is a friend? No, *we* can't, but Jesus can – He does! Like Dante, we probably think his treachery deserves one of the remoter parts of Hell, and yet knowing the worst, Jesus still calls him His friend. Though all that was in the heart of Judas was clear to Jesus at the Last Supper, He would not break the bond of friendship that He had made with him. In Jewish culture, to dip the bread and share it with a guest, as Jesus does with Judas, is to celebrate the gift of friendship, and to bind oneself afresh to a deep bond with that friend. Even as He marks him out to the others as His betrayer, Jesus commits Himself to His friend, His words echoing those of Psalm 41: 'Thus even my friend, in whom I trusted, who ate my bread, has turned against me.' (*Ps* 41:10). But more than this, when Judas approaches Jesus in the garden – even when he would betray Him with a kiss – Jesus says: 'Friend, why are you here?'

I can't tell you the full significance of those loving words for us. That even at the pinnacle of betrayal, even when He is to be abused with a hollow kiss, Jesus will not deny His friend, but through him names all who betray Him as friend, my friend. Judas represents the dark mystery of our sin in all its starkness – illogical, unnecessary, self-indulgent. And in the face of this sin, Jesus remains faithful and loving. As one writer puts it:

> As for Jesus, He closed His eyes to it and allowed time and grace to take their course. Before that heart which was gradually closing itself against Him, He opened up the treasures of His forbearance; He was prodigal in His forgiveness, that rare and precious gift we are nearly always reluctant to bestow.

A priest who taught me in school used to say that the saddest line in the whole of Scripture was when the Creator said to the created: 'better that you had never been born.'

It's true these lines are tragic, but I don't understand them now as I did then. The tragedy lies not in Judas's evil deed, but in the fact that he frustrates the creative love of his Friend; a love that would transform him and make possible the destiny for which he was born – a place of peace and joy closest to the Father's heart. Not to be born again to this place through the love of Jesus makes a nonsense of human life. Without the possibility of this goal, it would be better had we not been born.

What Judas teaches us is that there is nothing we can do that will stop Jesus from loving us. This man, whose treachery is certainly great, freely chooses to put himself beyond the love of Jesus – a love which, despite all his choices, never stops. What St Paul tries to teach us in his beautiful words to the Romans, Judas shows us in all its reality:

> For I am certain of this: neither death nor life, no angel, no prince, nothing that exists, nothing still to come, not any power, nor height nor depth, nor any created thing, can ever come between us and the love of God made visible in Christ Jesus our Lord (*Rom* 8:38-39).

There is something else that we can learn from Judas which will help us in our friendship with Jesus. It will help us because it teaches us about ourselves. Judas is not just the dark contrast that shows up the radiant love of Jesus. Through Judas, the New Testament also teaches us something profound about the mystery of sin – of our sin. Call to mind three sinful actions of Judas: first, he betrays Jesus – accepts money for Him; second, he tells the authorities of His whereabouts in the garden so they can arrest Him; and third, he identifies Him with a kiss. Three clear deeds of darkness, it would seem, but when we begin to look at how the Gospel writer presents these sins, we see that they are more complex, more mysterious than they first seem.

The New Testament describes Judas's betrayal as a 'handing over'. Judas hands over his Friend to the chief priests and scribes, but so, too, do the Scriptures describe the handing over of Jesus into the hands of sinful men as the will of the Father. Again, the word that St Luke uses to describe how Judas informs the authorities of Jesus's whereabouts can also mean to confess with praise – while Judas informs the authorities with a formal complaint, he also confesses Jesus, gives praise to Him. And of course, the kiss. Can we really distinguish the kiss of peace from the kiss of betrayal? Can Judas? It seems that all the sinful actions of Judas are not unadulterated darkness. Mysteriously within each one, there is a paradoxical echo of God's will for the good. As Graham Greene said in his novel *The End of the Affair*:

Hatred seems to operate the same glands as love: it produces the same actions. If we had not been taught how to interpret the Passion – would we have been able to say, from their actions alone, whether it was the jealous Judas or the cowardly Peter who loved Christ?

The English mystic Julian of Norwich said an unusual thing: that it was disclosed to her by the Lord Jesus, in one of her revelations, that: 'our sin shall be our glory.' For her, it's as if when we sin we keep getting things back-to-front and inside out. Doesn't St Paul say in his Letter to the Romans, 'For I do not do what I want, but I do the very thing I hate' (*Rom* 7:15 (RSV))? As if sin is a deformed, misshapen, frustrated effort at good. And if, like Judas's kiss, we examined our sin, we would see in it the frustrated deeper desire for good. Mother Julian believed that one day all our bundled, misguided, and sinful actions, all our failures, will be unravelled by the love of God and purified so that our often-hidden longing to do his will shall become clear – shall be our glory.

Why Julian of Norwich can proclaim that 'all shall be well and all shall be well and all manner of things shall be well' is because she believes that, fundamentally, even our efforts to sin are somehow marked by the goodness of our creation: sins are ugly corruptions of the very things we were made to do and really want to do. Just as with Judas, hidden in all our betrayals is a frustrated confession of His name. Only by moving closer to the light of Jesus, to the power of His Resurrection, can we see our sin and ourselves aright, begin to see that if we freely turn in this very weakness, His power will be made perfect. Judas did not turn.

Nicodemus (*John* 3:1-21)

When he began his pontificate, Benedict XVI said some beautiful words:

> If we let Christ into our lives, we lose nothing, nothing, absolutely nothing of what makes life free, beautiful, and great. No! Only in this friendship are the doors of life opened wide. Only in this friendship is the great potential of human existence truly revealed. Only in this friendship do we experience beauty and liberation.

We have all had a glimpse of how true the late Pope's words are; but we all know too how difficult, how frightening it can be, to let Christ into our lives. Rather than losing nothing, we tend to feel we will lose a great deal, not least our freedom. Sometimes, we need a little loving encouragement as we try to let Christ into our sinful lives more and more; as we try to let go of all that holds us back and to follow Him in freedom. The story of Nicodemus, a friend of Jesus who felt he had a lot to lose, might provide us with the encouragement we need.

Nicodemus is a Pharisee, he's a leader, a member of the Sanhedrin, and John tells us that he first comes to Jesus by night in the dark so he can't be seen. He sneaks up to

Jesus by night because he is attracted, he's seen the signs and heard his message, but he doesn't want this to disturb his day job. What is revealing is that this Teacher calls Jesus 'Rabbi'. Hidden within this is a suggestion that he could become a disciple.

Poor Nicodemus. Don't we all find ourselves with him sometimes – compromised – attracted by Jesus but still bound by all the things that are important to us like appearing to be wise and holy, being in with the right people who have security and power, being comfortable. But there is no compromise with Jesus – the choice is clear: it's either the old regime or the Kingdom and that cannot be simply an external thing, just a matter of following the signs. You must be born again. When it comes down to it, there must be a personal inner choice for the Spirit and against the flesh. Either we choose the security of wealth, power, prestige, whatever, or the freedom of the Spirit, who cannot be controlled but who blows where He will. But poor Nicodemus cannot quite bring himself to consider his own personal discipleship – he continually talks of 'we': 'we know that you are a teacher'. What Jesus is looking for is something quite simple, something that He found on the shore of the lake: a personal response that states clearly, 'I want to follow you. I want to live according to Your Kingdom – and I will.'

There are lots of similarities between Nicodemus and us 'professional religious'. How often do we stand secure behind the 'we' of the Church, the 'we' of our community? Oh yes, we believe, we follow Jesus, we work for his Kingdom. And how often does all the security that comes with our lives in the Church mean that we rarely think of surrendering our own self, rarely think of making a personal commitment to Jesus and His Kingdom? Our choice is as momentous and significant as that of Nicodemus. It's a choice the Lord asks of us every day, as we open the door to leave our room in the morning. He asks us to agree to be born again. Are our morning prayers just going to be what we do, or through them are we acknowledging the Spirit that has been planted in our heart and that unites us with our community so that, together, we can make the Kingdom come? If each of us says 'yes' to that Spirit, our lives will testify to what we have seen and, even though that might only mean a smile or a kind word, people will accept our testimony and believe.

We next meet Nicodemus when the ruling council are angry that Jesus seems to be beguiling the people with His words, and they insist on His arrest (*John* 7:45-52). Then, Nicodemus – who we are told first went to Jesus by night – makes a public stand by asking: 'Does our law condemn a man without first hearing him?' For this he's accused of being a Galilean. 'Does our law?' Nicodemus comes forward from within his group and makes a stand for Jesus. It seems that the challenge that Nicodemus received from Jesus at night, a challenge caught up in the gentle chiding of a friend: 'You a teacher in Israel and you do not know these things!' might be taking effect. 'Are you a Galilean too?' Nicodemus is asked by his fellow Pharisees, and straight away we hear an echo of the question put to Peter in the courtyard – put while Nicodemus and the Council are trying Jesus for His life. Then Peter betrays Him. Then Nicodemus is silent. At the critical moment, neither Peter nor Nicodemus fully commit to their Friend.

After this brief stand for justice, Nicodemus, as a member of the ruling council, is complicit in Jesus's death and condemnation. It is true that after Jesus is dead – safely out of the way – he reappears again, but once again by night, to perform the kind deed of Christ's burial. Sadly he's gone back to the shadows.

The story of Nicodemus is full of the ambiguity that marks our own life. It tells of the attraction of Jesus, of efforts to live in the light but ultimately of a return to the shadows and to security. How comforting it should be to us that all of our weak efforts and backsliding are embodied by a friend who has already brought them before the Lord. Perhaps we could just take two things from the friendly encounter between our Saviour and the Pharisee. First and foremost, we should notice the patience and gentleness of Jesus, the graciousness with which He meets this man, the understanding that He shows him. Jesus speaks the truth to him and waits lovingly for his rebirth. It's the Lord's patience which provides Nicodemus's opportunity to be saved, and it's our opportunity too.

And that's the second point that the story might teach: in His patience, God offers continuous opportunities for us to be saved, to be born again. No matter how often or how seriously we fail, another opportunity is given. Jesus never closes the door of friendship to us. What is good about the story of Nicodemus is that we do not know the end. Yes, like Peter, Nicodemus failed to identify himself personally with Jesus when it mattered, but who knows if he returned to the tomb after the Sabbath and heard from Mary of how to be born again.

Mary of Magdala (*John* 20:11-1-18)

Judas, Nicodemus and, finally, Mary of Magdala. I really like these three characters, not only because in them I know that Jesus has already met all my sin and weakness, but because the three of them offer increasing hope to us – hope that our Friend and Saviour, Jesus Christ, who has overcome the darkness of this life once and for all, will make His eternal light shine on us.

Let's look to Mary Magdalene to learn how that Easter light will come to us. Well, her story begins with sadness and weeping. Her story begins in darkness, among the dead, near the tomb. Four times we are told of Mary's tears, of her weeping. In fact, the theme of tears and searching occupies the entire first half of this Easter story. Listening to the Gospel, we can't fail to recall the words of the Song of Songs: 'I sought him whom my heart loves. I sought but did not find him. So I will rise and go through the City; in the streets and the squares I will seek him whom my heart loves.' (*Song* 3:1-2). This is the theme of the search for God which marks the whole of the Scriptures – the whole of humanity: 'O God, you are my God, for you I long' (*Ps* 63 (62)), and the words of another song are echoed here too: 'My tears have become my bread, by night, by day, as I hear it said ll the dy long: "Where is your God?"'(*Ps* 42). The description that we have in the Gospel and all the references that it evokes in our mind make it clear that Mary Magdalene, apparently being described as an individual with her own particular characteristics, in fact symbolises the whole of humankind weeping, because we are deprived of God and ceaselessly searching for Him.

Mary Magdalene is like us in another way too – her search, like ours, is often somewhat misdirected. Her search, like ours, is being conducted in human terms. Like Nicodemus, Mary has returned to the past – even when Jesus makes Himself present, she cannot get beyond the Jesus she knew – she's so fixed on the death of Jesus that it's impossible for her to entertain consolation or the fact that Jesus could be present to her in a new way. It is something similar that causes us all to refuse consolation and remain in the disappointment of sin. We block ourselves to any possibility of a new life, a new reality, and constantly return to the past, to past hurts and past mistakes. Just as Mary didn't want to be consoled and persisted in her desire for the Lord's dead body, so, too, we have difficulty in accepting the transforming joy that is there for us.

Think back to another woman who refused to be comforted – a woman who is mentioned when Jesus makes His first exodus – when He escapes Herod to leave Egypt for Nazareth. Then, St Matthew uses this unusual text:

> A voice is heard in Ramah,
> lamentation and bitter weeping.
> Rachel is weeping for her children;
> she refuses to be comforted for her children,
> because they are no more. (*Jer* 31:15/*Matt* 2:18)

How many of us live a little bit like Rachel, like Mary, refusing to be comforted: looking to the past to when there were more believers, larger numbers, more priests, sisters, young people? Like Mary, we are looking for Him amongst what was – not being open to the fact that He has gone before us into Galilee, and not being faithful to the fact that He promised to be with us always. This is what Mary must tell her brothers – tell the Church – that a new life that we cannot yet imagine has been brought about by Christ and is changing the world already. That is Resurrection faith – and faith in the Resurrection is hard.

How does the light of Resurrection come to Mary and to us? Well, the Resurrection of the incarnate Son of God is not revealed by the announcement of the event: 'I have risen!' It is not trumpeted by our Saviour, but the fact is communicated by the uttering of a friend's name. Cardinal Martini tells us that we should never cease to marvel at this – that the solemn event of Resurrection, the turning point of the whole of history, is conveyed in the simple and intimate conversation of two friends, a conversation which is built around such common human experiences as tears and weeping. But there is a reason why the news of Resurrection comes to us in this way – the revelation is so personal, so particular to each one of us, that hearing it makes us suddenly aware of who we are in the sight of God. We are children of the Father who now can share the place which Jesus has – because his Father is our Father. Judas could not accept this, and Nicodemus struggled to be born to a new life in the Spirit, but Mary, when she hears her name, welcomes the new life of Easter as her own.

When Mary turns at the sound of her name, she turns to the light. She's no longer looking to the past, to all that had gone wrong – now Jesus invites her to turn to the future. The aching search of humanity is ended in the encounter of the New Man and the New Woman in the garden, on the first day of the week. Estrangement, brought about in the garden at the beginning, is reconciled in the gentle call of a name. We too, if we listen, can hear the Lord call our name, and we can leave our past and all its hurt and embrace the light which He has made eternal. Jesus, through His friend Mary Magdalene, has shown us that we are all reconciled.

Week Three: What Jesus Sees in His Friends – Martha, Mary, and Lazarus

I'd like to begin today's reflection with an excerpt from a book I read a few years ago. It's from a book of essays on friendship, written by a man named Andrew, who was suffering from HIV. I suppose it's about his discovering the friendship of Jesus through his own friends, and in a way, through Martha, the friend of Jesus. He writes of the time that he began to tell his friends that he was dying:

> …and I told him the news. And it took a few seconds for it to sink in, but as it did, his face collapsed and he said quite simply, and quite clearly, 'Andrew, Andrew,' and in the timbre of his words, and in the repetition of the name and in the mixture of concern and disappointment, shock, and warmth, I recognised at once the voice, instantly and shockingly, and I recognised the tone. And then, a few days later still, this time on the phone, another person in my life responded to the news in exactly the same way – 'Andrew, Andrew' – a lament, an invitation, a sudden acknowledgement of what had, until then, been undetectable. And I heard it again; and I knew where it was from.
>
> And then a few days later; when for the first time I actually sat down and prayed, I found myself with a

copy of the Bible, and like some schoolboy, flipping through it for some sort of comfort, I came haphazardly upon the end of Luke's Chapter 10. And this is what I found myself reading:

> Now as they went on their way, Jesus entered a village. And a woman named Martha welcomed him into her house. And she had a sister called Mary, who sat at the Lord's feet and listened to his teaching. But Martha was distracted with much serving. And she went up to him and said, "Lord, do you not care that my sister has left me to serve alone? Tell her then to help me." But the Lord answered her, "Martha, Martha, you are anxious and troubled about many things, but one thing is necessary. Mary has chosen the good portion, which will not be taken away from her."

'Martha, Martha.' I don't think Jesus ever speaks to anyone else in the Gospels that way. 'Martha, Martha.' He repeats the name twice, exasperated but loving, admonitory but intimate. It's one of those many details that convince me that so much of the Gospels is true, the kind of intimate, intensely personal way of speaking, a detail that would never have been invented by someone trying to bludgeon the reader into some didactic lesson, the kind of address that a real person once used to a real person, and a real person He loved, as much as for her faults as in spite of them. 'Martha, Martha.' 'Andrew, Andrew.' It is not the tone simply of love; it is the tone of friendship, an unmistakable tone, a tone that I did not only recognise, but suddenly, heartbreakingly, knew (Andrew Sullivan, *Love Undetectable*, 30-32).

So, one man hears with certainty the friendly voice of Jesus addressed to him personally through the words of the Gospel. We can hear that voice today, too, but perhaps it will strike us more deeply if we reflect on just what it is in Martha that evokes such a loving response from Christ. Today, we will contemplate what Jesus sees in His friends and we'll reflect on His three friends from Bethany; the only ones that the Gospels specifically say He loved – knowing why He loved them should help us to accept that He loves us too – should make us certain of His friendly words in our lives.

Martha (*Luke* 10:38-42, *John* 11:17-27)

In the Gospels, St John, in particular, confronts us with what Cardinal Martini calls 'a gallery of portraits of friends of the Lord', and each friend, he says, is there to add some insight, to increase the depth of our own intimacy with the Word amongst us. Amongst the evangelists, it is John who speaks of Jesus's love for Martha, Mary, and Lazarus; John who calls them His friends. While there are shades of Luke's portrayal of Martha and Mary, in John things are different. John, like Luke, does present two aspects of

discipleship through these women, but here it's different
from the active/contemplative presentation. In John, we
get a fuller sense of this woman Martha, and why Jesus
would love her.

Martha is the friend who meets you on familiar terms.
She speaks openly and simply, in a conversation that exudes
attention and trust. Think of the Samaritan woman, or the
woman with the haemorrhage who we considered earlier –
think of their approach to Jesus, and then think of Martha.
The Samaritan woman is full of worries and tells her tale
to Jesus only with reluctance and reserve. She is hesitant
and tries not to give herself away – she avoids touching on
fundamental points.

In contrast, think of the conversations that you know of
Martha: St Luke has her say: 'Lord, do you not care that my
sister is leaving me to do the serving all by myself?' Surely,
it's partly this frankness, this honesty, which draws from
Jesus His 'Martha, Martha.' Often, it's hard to imagine the
tone of what Jesus is saying, it can be difficult to picture His
face as He speaks His words, but that's not true here: to me
these words hold a bit of laughter, they are loving and full
of affection. Clearly, Martha is happy to speak her mind
and to hear the thoughts of others without fuss. But it's in
John, perhaps, that we hear her greatest frankness: 'Lord, if
you had been here, my brother would not have died. And
now I know that whatever you ask from God, God will give
you.' (*John* 11:21-22, RSV). Martha is frank and open – she

says easily what's on her mind – she is familiar because she trusts her Friend, and knows that whatever she says He will love her. That doesn't make her reckless or unthinking, it makes her upfront and confident in a way which Jesus clearly loves.

Perhaps we've spent too much time considering Martha as a busy domestic instead of a woman who makes others comfortable because she is frank and open. The welcome that Martha gives to Jesus in her home is one that makes Him relax, it makes Him return because He finds a place of love and ease.

What can we learn from Martha? Well, obviously, we can learn from her confidence and openness. To speak what is in our heart directly and honestly is what a friend does, and it is what we should do with Jesus. But we could notice, too, that the scenes in which Martha appears in the Gospel are scenes of tension. She is busy serving, she is busy coping with the death of her brother and all the mourners. Martha seems to keep her head through this tension because she relies on Him like one does on an old friend with whom we share all. By doing this, she shows complete trust that all that is on her mind is interesting and important to the Lord. So in times of tension we, too, should be certain of the friendly ear of the Lord; certain of Someone, who, with humour and love, will repeat our name and lead us from all that worries and threatens us to a place of calm friendship and peace.

Mary (*Luke* 10:38-42, *John* 12:1-8)

Mary is the one who takes the 'better part' at the feet of the Lord. Her reserve and equanimity contrast with Martha. Unlike Martha, who seems attractive to Jesus because she goes out to meet Him directly and on friendly terms, Mary meets Him as His disciple, sat at His feet. And yet we don't imagine that she's positioned at Christ's feet in subservience but in love. He is the one who has come to serve, the one who says the greatest is the least, but as is common, friends want to be like the one they are attracted to. Mary wants to be with Jesus, she's captivated by Him and wants to spend time listening and understanding Him. Though by different means to her sister, Mary wants to offer Jesus a place where He can relax and open up –unlike her sister's straight-talking ebullience, it's Mary's reflective silence which brings forth His words and affection. What Jesus seems to find attractive in Mary is her silence, her attentive posture, and her effort to learn to be like Him.

In John's Gospel, there is another scene where Mary of Bethany is prominent. It's a scene in which we get a sense of her lavish generosity – a scene in which there is certainly no fasting, but where the Bridegroom is anointed with a large amount of costly ointment – a pound of pure nard. Now, perhaps, we glimpse something more of the seemingly quiet Mary – her freedom and her confidence. She is in no way inhibited in her gift or in her actions. She kisses Jesus, washes His feet, and wipes them with her hair. Perhaps her hours of quiet listening and conversation have brought her to this point. Jesus will not have her criticised though. He insists that she be left alone. This woman makes a simple lavish gift and Jesus is delighted by it.

In seeking a symbol to show how Christ is the centre of our life, we too want more than words. Just like Mary of Bethany, who broke her precious alabaster vase, we seek acts which proclaim that we give all that we are to Christ. We've each of us made such a symbolic act in the Church when we broke our life open for Him in Baptism, through Marriage, Profession or Ordination, but we need to think of ways to renew that gift by breaking our jars from day to day. We might, one day, break from our going-through-the-motions prayers and for once make them patient, loving, and trusting – poured out in praise. We might break from a laziness, which means we are content to repeat received words and ideas. Instead, we might seek to deepen their meaning by making them our own – a personal gift to our Friend. We might try to break from all that keeps us from dedicating ourselves fully to Christ.

Breaking something of our own will be a sacrifice that costs us. We will have to surrender, and others are watching and wondering. It demands courage. But all that was true of our friend in the Gospel, who entered Simon's house and, regardless of everyone, broke open her perfumed gift. Somehow, our friend Mary gives us courage to go forward, to step out and to make our journey to the Lord's feet. For us, breaking the alabaster jar is a daily way of saying 'yes' to our life's calling; of saying with joy 'See, Lord, I'm not turning back.'

Lazarus (*John* 11:1-16; 11:38-45)

And finally, Lazarus. His sisters describe him to Jesus as 'the one you love', and when they request Jesus to return because their brother is sick, He does eventually leave His mission to return to Bethany. Who knows? Maybe there is something of a psychological struggle in Jesus during these days, but friendship eventually wins out. Even the Kingdom can wait for Lazarus, it seems. Of all the friends of Jesus, perhaps with the exception of the Beloved Disciple, John, Lazarus is the most significant. Certainly, what he teaches us about what Jesus sees in His friends is of the utmost importance.

You see, whereas in other cases we can discern some motive for the love of Jesus – Martha is lively, frank, bustling; Mary poised, collected, and lavish – in the case of Lazarus, it is difficult to answer the questions: what aspect of friendship is stressed here, or what is it that attracts Jesus in this man? That's because Lazarus, in fact, does nothing, says nothing. We don't really know anything about him. In the Gospels, he has no developed character. And yet, Lazarus is the one whom the Gospels tell us Jesus was closest to, changed His plans for, shed tears for, risked death for. Well now! If we want to perceive, to read in the Gospels an aspect of friendship that Lazarus makes clear, we must say that it's the fact that he does nothing – and that's the point, for in this friendship Jesus does everything.

Lazarus teaches the most important thing we need to learn about the friends of Jesus. It's that Jesus decides. It's Jesus who chooses His friends. There is no need to find some other special characteristic because the first, most basic characteristic of friendship is freedom: all friends are freely chosen. Yes, there might be something that catches the eye or draws the attention, but at the end of the day beauty is in the eye of the beholder; and the beholder is absolutely free to decide what's beautiful for him or herself. Of all the characters in the New Testament, Lazarus represents the person that Jesus loves, simply because Jesus wants to. All Lazarus needs to do is simply accept.

In the end, as we contemplate these friends from Bethany, we might do well to wonder whether they are not all more alike than we think. After all, they are a family of friends. Maybe the friendships that each of them has with Jesus are not separate or distinct, but merely aspects that the evangelist has drawn out for effect – aspects that every friend of Jesus possesses more or less. Perhaps, then, I put the cart before the horse in this reflection. We should have started with Lazarus first, because now it seems to me that knowing Jesus has chosen you as a friend – for reasons known only to His heart and not to anyone else –

should give you enormous confidence. To know that each one of us is chosen and loved, unconditionally, gives us the confidence and energy to be free, to be ourselves. And that's what Mary and Martha are – free to speak openly, to caress, to question, to kiss. So then, before we consider in our meditation how we might express our love of Jesus in our unique way, we should, without doubt, first meditate on His free and gratuitous choice of us, because when all is said and done, it is this loving choice which makes us free to break open our own perfume before Him or to tell Him our own tale.

If you would like to contemplate these characters today, think of each of them as you, but though it might be a funny thing to say, imagine yourself as Lazarus. Imagine your surprise and delight that this most popular Wonder Worker has chosen you, comes to your house and enjoys your company. Try to be convinced, today, of the absolute choice God has made for you in Christ. He came to be your Friend as if you were the only person in the world, and, in these days, He will prove it to you. As André Louf said: 'What counts is that we entrust ourselves to His love, a love which is always the first to choose.'

Week Four: Friendships Forged in
Forgiveness – Zacchaeus and Peter

Well, we've spoken a lot about our sinfulness and about how the friendship of Jesus draws sinners out from darkness and isolation. Now, I'd like to talk about what difference that should make to us: what difference forgiveness and reconciliation make. First, I'd like to talk about Jesus's friend Zacchaeus. He's a fleeting character who meets Jesus in the street, and through that momentary encounter becomes His companion. Fleeting, but a favourite. People love this Gospel story, especially children. There's something delightful about this person and something simple and wonderful about the friendship he develops with the Lord. And then we could spend a while reflecting on the Apostle Peter. His friendship with Jesus is perhaps the most developed relationship in the Gospel, and through its twists and turns we witness the making of a solid bond. Both friendships are forged from forgiveness.

Zaccheus (*Luke* 19:1-10)

Zacchaeus was a Jew, but his life was compromised by what he did – he collected taxes for the Romans, an occupying power. Obviously, he would be despised for this, treated as an outsider, never trusted. There are shades of Judas here, aren't there? A traitor and untrustworthy money man. It would be par for the course for this man to up the taxes in order to cream off the excess for himself. Because he was short, as well as a tax collector, I'm sure there were a whole host of insults hurled at him, most beginning with, 'You thieving little…' No wonder he was good at climbing trees! Literally, St Luke introduces him as 'a man who called himself Zacchaeus', and perhaps that's because nobody else did. There were insults but no name: in the eyes of others, he was less than human; a nobody. Because of this, it's hard for Zacchaeus to know who he is himself. Maybe this is why Zacchaeus also has a desire to know what kind of man Jesus is. Perhaps he'd heard that this Man is a Friend of tax collectors and sinners, perhaps in his isolation he harboured the wild hope that Jesus would sit at his table – be his Companion, his Friend.

But did Jesus want to see Zacchaeus? It seems so. It's true Zacchaeus doesn't give Jesus much option, positioning himself right in His eye line, like a target. Jesus only had to raise His eyes to look straight into the eyes of Zacchaeus. In that moment, quite a few things change for Zacchaeus, and they should for us too. The man who's used to being looked down on, the man who expects to be called anything but his name, who is normally shunned and met with an angry face, is here looked up to by Jesus, who calls him Zacchaeus, looks at him lovingly and seeks his company. What did Zacchaeus feel in that moment? He felt reconciled, he felt forgiven, and he felt joy. And has this

Gospel changed how we see the God who reconciles? Don't we tend to assume that God would look down on us when we fail? Don't we expect that we'll have to give an account of all we've done when we meet, and then in His mercy He will allow us back? This is not the way of Jesus. Salvation comes when – exactly *because* of our shortcomings – we are a source of attraction to the Lord, are raised up in His sight and looked upon with love and compassion. There is no condemnation, no condescension here. And yet the question remains for us sinners: whether it's harder for us to meet the upward, laughing, glance of love and move on – or to stay frozen under the downcast eyes of reproach that we have been conditioned to expect.

In that tree, Zacchaeus was as he was: a sad customer, a miserable little traitor. Right up until the moment that Jesus engages him with the eyes of the Father – eyes that make no distinction but look on the evil and the righteous with the same love. It's this gaze that brings an unexpected peace to this anxious little man. And this peace turns to joy when Jesus is willing not only to meet him, but to stay with him and eat with him – Jesus literally becomes Zacchaeus's companion, He shares his bread. And what does this reconciliation mean? It means that Zacchaeus is given his life back: given a restoration that causes him to return the life he'd stolen from others.

It's worthwhile considering what forgiveness means for us: how we feel once reconciled with Jesus, whether we have anything of the peace, joy and new life which Zaccheus experiences. Do we have the humility to let Jesus look up to us as He did to Zaccheus; the humility to be loved by Him or do we want to maintain that degree of separation from Jesus which means nothing is asked of us: no new beginning or new life. The forgiveness and reconciliation that happens between us and Jesus is that of friends – little Zaccheus teaches us that.

The best explanation of God's anger I ever received was from a teacher who used the image of a mirror. When we stand before a mirror and look at our reflection, it seems that the mirror has depth; that our distance from the mirror's surface is reflected on the other side. The further we move away from the mirror, the further our image seems to retreat into the mirror. But this is an illusion because the mirror is flat and stationary. It just appears that our image vanishes as we move away. My teacher compared what the Scriptures call God's anger to this 'distance' in the mirror. As we move away from God, it just appears that God takes His distance from us. The anger of God is something manufactured on our side. It results from our movements, not from God's. God, in fact, is constant, unchanging love – like the surface of the mirror, God does not move. As Zaccheus strayed from God and God's commands, it seemed that God had taken His distance from him, that God was angry with him. In his encounter with Jesus at the bottom of that tree, Zacchaeus discovered a true reflection of God and of himself. He learned in that moment of forgiveness that God is love, and so can we.

Peter (*John* 18:15-27; 21:15-20)

This firm friendship, this rock-like love, is something that Peter discovers in Jesus too. The Dominican priest Fr Simon Tugwell says something very important about St Peter. He says: 'In different ways, all of us live off the faith of Peter, the Rock upon which Christ builds His Church.' What makes Peter's faith in Jesus, his Friend, rock-like is forgiveness. Peter's experience of the friendship of Jesus, through forgiveness and reconciliation, is so strong and profound – so like a rock – that it strengthens us: it makes our faith and our friendship with the Lord solid too. Peter is chosen to be the one who strengthens his brethren because he himself knew what it was to be strengthened. Let's look a little bit at his friendship with the Lord – especially at how we can learn to deepen our friendship with Jesus through His gift of forgiveness to us, through reconciliation.

Fr Simon says we should begin with the words of Jesus:

Simon, Simon! Satan, you must know, has got his wish to sift you all like wheat; but I have prayed for you, Simon, that your faith may not fail, and once you have recovered, you in your turn must strengthen your brothers. (*Luke* 22:31-32)

'You in your turn' – it is almost that in and through the repentance and reconciliation of Peter – in his 'turn' – we will find strength. In this phrase, too, we cannot fail but notice that gentle and familiar tone which the Lord used with His friend Martha: 'Martha, Martha!' But there's more here. What is remarkable about this passage is what someone called 'the utterly casual way in which Jesus refers to Peter's sin', to his betrayal. In fact, Jesus only implies the sin through Peter's act of repentance and conversion: 'once you have recovered'. This is the perspective that Jesus takes on our sins. Jesus, who knows and sees everything about us. Before Peter has even committed the sin, Jesus is already looking at it from the perspective, from the point of view, of reconciliation and peace. Jesus is already, and always, looking on our sins as a thing of the past – that's the perspective He takes – even before we come to confess to Him. Such is the depth and strength of His friendship with us: for Him, a break in our relationship is unimaginable!

As I've said previously, in the words of Julian of Norwich, Peter's sins are already regarded by Jesus as his future glory. His sins, once healed and reconciled by Christ, are what make him a rock and a means of strength for his brethren. They say that scar tissue which forms after a wound is much stronger, don't they? Let's look first at Peter's denials, and then at Peter reconciled with Christ and strong. To do this, we'll go first to the Mount of Olives, and then to the Garden of Gethsemane.

On the Mount of Olives, Peter sees a Jesus he has never met before, a Jesus he does not recognise. He encounters One filled with anguish – distressed, fearful, and sweating blood. Here, for the first time, Peter sees Jesus overcome by weakness, and this was not his Messiah. Peter had come to fight; he had brought his sword to battle for the Kingdom, and here he is confronted with a Lord wrapped in fear, quaking. When they come to arrest Jesus, Peter gives one last cry to his mighty Hero: 'Lord, shall we use the sword?' only to be told by Jesus, 'Leave off! That will do!' Though Jesus had tried to teach Peter of His Kingdom and of its coming through His suffering and death, Peter would not accept. Now, in the garden, all his hopes are shattered.

As a result, Peter falls into a great confusion – a confusion as to who Jesus is and who he is himself. This helps us all the better to understand his denials! Peter follows his Master but keeps himself at a distance. Then, he is confronted by the words of the first accuser: 'This one was with Him.' Peter gives the answer: 'Woman, I don't know Him' – a denial, yes, but also the truth. Peter does not know this weak and fearful Lord. This Man is not the Jesus Peter had followed and come to believe in. The Jesus Peter knew was a strong leader, a winner, his Master. Then, Peter is confronted again: 'You were one of them,' and he denies it saying: 'No, I'm not the man.' Without his Lord, Peter cannot imagine his own identity. This is a similar dynamic to that which we saw in the story of Zacchaeus. Only in the light of Jesus do His friends discover who they really are, and, when they fail to grasp the identity of Jesus, they fail to know or understand themselves. *Gaudium et Spes* teaches the truth of this when it says in paragraph 22: 'only in the mystery of the incarnate Word does the mystery of man take on light.'

This is the deeper meaning of 'No, I am not the man.' If Peter does not know Christ, he cannot know himself. Here are the tragic twists and turns of someone who had generously begun to follow the way of his Friend, but who now no longer understands either Jesus or himself. How often do we find this to be true of us? Then comes Peter's third denial. The accuser says, 'He was with him; he too is a Galilean.' But Peter replies: 'Sir, you do not know what you are saying!' Peter's trial is one of the most terrible a person could suffer. In it, we see Peter's very self, and his whole world, collapse. His identity, origin, relationships are gone without Jesus, he is without every meaningful compass point in life. All he had put his hopes on is gone. And as he had said himself: 'to whom and where shall we go?' Without Jesus, there is nothing and nowhere. Peter then had come to the point of doubting and denying everything – everything that the Lord had said, everything that had formed their friendship.

If Peter passed through this trial, he passed through it for the whole Church, for us, to strengthen us, as Jesus foretold. Peter stands in sharp contrast to Judas. Yes, he betrays his Master, by denying Him, but he 'recovers' in a way that

Judas doesn't. He weeps bitterly over what he has done – and so, his darkness is creative. In the moment when he meets the eyes of Jesus across the courtyard – like Zacchaeus had met them in the busy street – he allows himself to be loved, reconciled, recreated. Now for the first time, he understands that before God he can do nothing other than let himself be loved, forgiven, saved, just in the way his Friend would have it, and not according to his own plans.

The story of the friendship between Jesus and Peter is carefully constructed in the New Testament. We know more about this friendship than any other. But the aspect of the friendship which is rendered with most detail and delicacy in the Scriptures is their reconciliation. The story is told by St John in the final chapter of his Gospel. Everything in the passage looks backward and forward. The setting of the charcoal fire is reminiscent of the High Priest's courtyard, the scene of the triple betrayal, but now it is Jesus who asks three questions of Peter. In Matthew's account of the Resurrection, the women are described hurrying away from the tomb 'afraid yet filled with joy'. It seems that reconciliation always entails this acute intersection of feelings. Isn't it partly fear that sends Zacchaeus up a tree, and joy that brings him down? Peter certainly is filled with joy as he sees the Man he loves on the lakeside, the Man who was his life. He must have been filled with fear too – to meet Jesus in the light of day, with all his weaknesses and sin exposed.

In the *Benedictus* that some of us pray each day in the Office, we hear of the 'loving kindness of the heart of our God who visits us like the dawn from on high.' Peter need not fear this visitation of the Son of the Most High God, who comes to him in the dawn-light on the shore of Tiberias. The day of the Lord's visitation was a feared day – a day of anger and wrath, but the visitation of Jesus to Peter is free from anger or revenge. It is here that we grasp the full meaning of God's awful visitation – of reconciliation. Yes, it is an inspection where every detail, every tiny deficiency is exposed to the light, but only so it can be supplied for, provided for out of God's mercy. This is what Jesus does with Peter. In this encounter, he is given back his life, his past, his self – but now completed, recreated, made new. This is why Peter becomes a rock, our rock.

By loving us Jesus reconciles us to ourselves and to Him. He gives our past back to us refined and purified, every lack made whole and strengthened for a new future. What is the end result of reconciliation with Jesus? St Peter teaches us. After Peter, quite upset, has professed his love for the third time, and Jesus commissions him to feed His sheep, the Lord adds: 'Follow me!' Peter has been given his life back by Jesus – renewed right back to their first meeting on another shore. Now, this 'follow me' is Peter's final calling: what Cardinal Martini calls his 'last Exodus'. Peter had experienced such a calling out – an exodus – before. It was when he witnessed the miraculous catch of fish (*Luke* 5:4-

11), and overcome at the prospect of such a new life he said: 'Leave me Lord, I am a sinful man.' Then he heard the words: 'Come, follow me, and I will make you a fisher of men' and he left everything.

Throughout the Gospel, there are many other moments when Jesus calls Peter – when He calls Peter to come to Him across the water, when He asks him, 'Will you go away too?' Each incident calls for a break with the past, and the whole life of Peter is composed of a succession of these breaks – little reconciliations and new commissions. In each of them, Jesus forgives his lack of faith, shows him what is missing, and invites him to go beyond himself.

In this last chapter of John's Gospel, Jesus speaks to Peter about the final break. How does Jesus define this 'last Exodus'? He contrasts 'activity' with 'passivity': 'When you were young you put on your own belt and walked where you liked.' Certainly, Peter had already lived through a period of difficult and tiring ministry – but basically he was active and free. Now, the moment has come for him to make a final transition: one which all human beings make. 'When you grow old, you will stretch out your hands, and somebody else will put a belt around you and take you where you would rather not go.' The final leap of faith, the last call, is not a move from one activity to another, but a move to recognise the passive presence of the Cross at the heart of all our activity.

Now, Peter will come to know, intimately, what it means to know the crucified Christ, who Himself had been taken where He would rather not go, and Who in weakness held out His arms. In Peter, there will be a repugnance and a resistance to do these things, just like that of the Lord that he saw in Gethsemane – but now, Peter is reconciled to the fact that this is done in love. Peter, reconciled and forgiven, is called into the privileged place of Christ's true friends: the place of total self-giving love – the place of the garden, the place of the Cross, the place of new life. It is for this that Jesus reconciles us: to join Him in His Passion and Resurrection, and to love Him there as a Friend, eternally.

WEEK FIVE: SPECIAL FRIENDS OF THE LORD –
HIS BELOVED DISCIPLE AND HIS MOTHER, MARY

I remember an argument between my Grandma and my Auntie Rita. Well, not so much an argument as a frank discussion – nobody could argue with Auntie Rita! Over the years, my Grandma had developed a custom that when she welcomed a new grandchild into the world she would buy them a Premium Bond. She'd buy another when they were baptised, and one for each subsequent birthday. Towards the end of her life, she became worried. The older grandchildren would have more Premium Bonds than the ones born recently. 'It's not right, Rita. I don't want to have favourites; I must love them all the same.' 'No, you're wrong, Mother,' said her wise daughter. 'You can't love them all the same because they're all different. Each one's a favourite.'

I've never forgotten auntie's lesson. We're each of us special in God's eyes, loved differently and uniquely. We are favoured and, in a sense, 'favourites', beloved disciples. It might seem strange to think about Our Lady and St John as exhibiting a friendship that we can enjoy – even stranger to think of Mary and her Son as friends. Yet, in a way, Jesus portrays His friends in this way when He says of his close disciples: 'Here are my mother and my brothers.'

For St Thomas Aquinas, a key characteristic of true friendship is that friends live together and enjoy a shared life. Interesting that at the foot of the Cross, Mary and John establish a common life, and that John 'made a place for her in his home.' Let's consider this 'place' first in the life of John, and then in Mary's life. It's a homely place, which we'll recognise, by now, as friendship.

The Beloved Disciple (*John* 13:21-30)

We all know of the mysterious figure of the Beloved Disciple, the one Jesus loved especially, but I wonder if we know that he represents our friendship with Jesus in its perfection? In all the friends we've thought about so far, we've seen the beginnings of friendship in its different aspects and its development in various situations, but in the disciple John we see this friendship come to maturity. If we welcome the mystery of Christ's friendship, if we are open to receive it, we too will enjoy the intimacy of a beloved disciple.

We can tell a lot about the friendship between Jesus and this particular disciple from a verse or two in the Fourth Gospel, where the evangelist describes his presence at the Last Supper. We are told that:

> The disciple Jesus loved was reclining next to Jesus; Simon Peter signed to him and said, 'Ask who it is he means,' so leaning back on Jesus's breast he said, 'Who is it, Lord?' (*John* 13:23-25)

In this short passage, the disciple takes up the place of friendship next to Jesus and closest to His heart. This phrase, 'leaning back on Jesus's breast' reminds us of how the same Gospel's prologue describes the place of Jesus in relation to the Father. There, we are told that He is the 'only Son, who is nearest to the Father's heart.' The beloved is as close to the heart of Jesus as Jesus is to the Father. To be a friend of Jesus means that we join Him in His place nearest the Father's heart. The Beloved Disciple has intuited this, he senses the mysteries that are stored up in the heart of Jesus – mysteries which Jesus pours out on His friends, and which will draw them to His Father's heart.

Friends always hold an element of mystery, don't they? We can never exhaust the full reality of a friend. There is always something more, something other, something else, and that's their beauty – that's the beauty of Jesus – a beauty which the Beloved Disciple, perhaps more than anyone, recognised. Jesus knew that this disciple was drawn to Him. He knew that this one sensed what was in His heart, and that's why he was beloved – and that's why we are too. What might we learn of the heart of Jesus from the disciple who lies next to Him at the Supper?

Imagine an egg timer – even better, an hour glass – and imagine the sand trapped in the upper chamber of the timer. Imagine the beautiful, swirling release of this fullness through the slim central channel. Almost incredible that such a delicate aperture could channel all in a single hour! According to the cosmic picture that we are given in the Fourth Gospel, all is likewise channelled in the hour of Jesus – the hour of His death on the Cross – when in His own flesh, out of His heart, a way was opened up, and all the blessings and promises of God, once restricted and held back by the rules and decrees of the Law, could flow down and be received by any human heart. In one beautiful, emptying movement, the Father gives us everything through the Son. Yet there is one point we can't afford to ignore in how these mysterious blessings come to us – a point that the apostle John knows very well.

The *Catechism* tells us that God loves us with a human heart – an open, human heart is what dispenses the mysteries. The open heart of Jesus is the delicate aperture from which all our promises and our blessings flow. What is unique to Christianity is that the saving plan of God hinges on the flesh – the human heart of Christ is the well from which we will draw the water of salvation with joy. This is what the Beloved Disciple came to know, it's what he teaches us. So, the one they call the Divine represents the friendship of the mature Christian – one who takes his or her place next to Jesus and basks in the love of the Father that is showered on them. We should all seek to be as beloved as he.

Perhaps you find all this a bit daunting or off-putting. How are us poor followers supposed to achieve the mystical heights of this Beloved Disciple? Well, perhaps it would help if we revealed his name. Over the years, scholars have suggested all sorts of people for the part of the Beloved.

Some have said he's Lazarus, some the rich young man who Jesus looked at steadily and loved, some have even said Judas. But most, together with the long tradition of the Church, say his name is John. And that's why we shouldn't be put off by the thought that this Beloved Disciple is some rare mystic.

In fact, he's one of the Twelve, who's elsewhere revealed as an ambitious, angry and intolerant character. He's one of Zebedee's sons, who ambitiously requests one of the best seats in the Kingdom; a Son of Thunder, who wants to call down fire on an unwelcoming Samaritan town; one who has a jealous heart when he sees another casting out devils in the Lord's name. How can this John be the one who rests meekly, close to the Lord's heart at His Last Supper? Haven't the Church and the exegetes chosen the wrong person? Well, no! This is the very point. John's whole life represents the change which friendship with Jesus can make – 'whereby', as Barclay says, 'the Son of Thunder did become the Apostle of Love'. The Beloved Disciple, John, should certainly be a friend of ours this Lent. He should be our inspiration: standing before us as a goal, teaching us what real friendship with Jesus can do, even to the least likely of characters. And he will surely sing with us this Easter of the unknown love of Jesus: 'Love to the loveless shown, that they might lovely be.'

Mary, the Mother of Jesus
(*Luke* 2:22-40, *John* 19:25-30)

In his encyclical letter, *Redemptoris Mater*, Pope St John Paul II says something about Mary that is very helpful as we try to negotiate this space, this place of friendship:

> One could perhaps speak of a specific 'geography' of faith and Marian devotion… Where the People of God seek to meet the Mother of God in order to find, in a certain 'place' within the maternal presence of her 'who believed,' a strengthening of their own faith. For in Mary's faith, first at the Annunciation and then fully at the foot of the Cross, an interior space was reopened within humanity which the Eternal Father can fill 'with every spiritual blessing' (*Redemptoris Mater*, 28).

It was the Protestant theologian Karl Barth who spoke of the virgin womb and the empty tomb as two bookends to the story of salvation. Mary initiates and stands by these spaces in her own life. And through her prayers, she keeps them open in the lives of believers, making possible the encounter of friendship that can take place there. This place becomes a space of shared life and friendship, and this is why we turn to her now, at this stage on our journey, as the ultimate exemplary friend of Jesus.

Think of Mary at Cana. Think of where she is, what she says, and how she acts. The Gospel says there was a wedding and 'the Mother of Jesus was there'. At the centre of the wedding feast of Cana is Mary – nobody could quibble with this – even Jesus and His disciples had only 'also been invited.' In relation to her, they are 'also/ands.' The figure of the mother is central for the evangelist. Mary is central.

And what does she do? How does she act? She observes, she watches, she studies everything. The Gospel tells us of a feast. We imagine a bustling scene of many people coming and going and doing different things – servants, waiters, guests, musicians, family, bride and groom. In this passage, no one, not even us, sees all. Only Mary observes every person, every detail of the scene, and like she has done previously, only she ponders on it. She literally synthesises the whole scene in her heart until she gets to know, until she perceives what is missing.

Mary takes in the whole scene, the bigger picture. She contemplates what she sees. She takes everything in and she considers, weighs, ponders. We often want to find fault. We scrutinise in order to diagnose and rectify. Here, Mary communicates the secret of comforting watchfulness: her contemplation displays a profound empathy and attentiveness to suffering. She stands by the empty space, she discerns amidst the business of life so as to shed light, speak truth, and collaborate with others.

Mary, our Mother, is still looking at us. From her vantage point in Heaven, she sees the whole of our life, from beginning to end. She ponders on it in her heart, in all its detail. Mary knows what is missing. The Mother, now caught up in Jesus's hour eternally, knows 'they have no wine.' For a while today, let's remain before the gaze of Mary, our Mother. Let's be willing to let her look compassionately at our whole life and allow her to discover what is missing: the empty place of friendship.

Commenting on this passage, Cardinal Martini says a very interesting thing. He says that what Mary points out as missing is not a matter of life and death; not something essential. What she recognises is 'a general lack of wellbeing, that indefinable something that makes all the difference – a source of joy.' Mary discovers and opens up the space of communion, of friendship with God that all the other characters we've reflected on have come to inhabit. She facilitates friendship between us and her Son: entry into the mysteries of a common life. She opens up a 'specific geography' for each one of us and allows us to take the place of a highly-favoured beloved disciple. She is the one who helps us both to imitate what this space can contain and to obtain what it promises. Like Miriam to the new Moses she brings us to the place where we say, 'Here I am' like she did: the holy ground where we take off our shoes and enjoy God's company – become God's intimate friend (*Ex* 3:4-6). In that space, the Lord will speak to us face to face and make known to us everything He has learnt from the Father (*Ex* 33:7-11; *John* 15: 12-16).

A Book of Welsh Bread

Bobby Freeman

Without our loyal supporters we would not be here today.

Help us respond to spiritual hunger

£10

£50

£150

Could provide four young people with booklets on prayer and vocation

Could help CTS invest in new catechesis materials for families

Could help us further develop our work with prison chaplaincies

CTS relies on the generosity of its supporters to carry out its mission.

SUPPORT US TODAY:

Call: +44 (0)20 7640 0042
Email: fundraising@ctsbooks.org
Go to: www.ctsbooks.org/give

God's truth beautifully told.
SINCE 1868.

Lent is a time to walk more closely with Jesus. In this book, Fr Philip Caldwell leads the reader through the season side by side with Our Lord, helping us to know him as his friends whilst on earth knew him. Perfect for parish groups or private devotion, over five weeks (or five days) the book introduces figures from the Gospels. For each Fr Philip recommends scripture passages to meditate upon and offers reflections to open the Gospels to us and allow us to approach Christ in friendship, deeper understanding and love.

We believe in helping people to discover, nurture and share their faith, by providing honest and compelling answers to life's deepest questions.

Everything we do is authentic, accessible, and authoritative. You can rely on us to tackle the important issues of life and faith, to make the complicated easy to understand, and that the work we publish is in line with the teachings of the Catholic Church.

As a charity and a publisher, we use the written word to support and encourage people at every stage of their journey; from parish priests to those exploring for the first time and from pre-schoolers to pensioners.

Catholic Truth Society
God's truth, beautifully told.
SINCE 1868

ISBN 978-1-78469-835-5

9 781784 698355

£3.95   D851

WWW.CTSBOOKS.ORG